KILLING FLOOR

Books by AI
CRUELTY (1973)
KILLING FLOOR (1979)

Killing Floor is the 1978 Lamont Poetry Selection of
the Academy of American Poets.

From 1954 through 1974 the Lamont Poetry Selection
supported the publication and distribution of twenty
first books of poems. Since 1975 this distinguished
award has been given for an American poet's second
book. Judges for 1978: Maxine Kumin, Philip Levine,
Charles Wright.

KILLING FLOOR

POEMS BY Ai

 1979

HOUGHTON MIFFLIN COMPANY BOSTON

Library of Congress Cataloging in Publication Data
Ai, date
  Killing floor

  I. Title.
PS3551.I2K5   811'.5'4   78-25663
ISBN 0-395-27593-8
ISBN 0-395-27590-3 pbk.

Printed in the United States of America

P 10 9 8 7 6 5 4 3 2 1

Most of the poems in this volume have previously appeared in various magazines, as follows:

Antaeus: "Father and Son," "He Kept On Burning," "The Kid," "The Singers," "The Gilded Man." *Black Box:* "Lesson, Lesson." *Chicago Review:* "Sleep Like a Hammer," "Ice." *Choice:* "Almost Grown." *Exile:* "The Mortician's Twelve-Year-Old Son," "Guadalajara Cemetery." *Iowa Review:* "Jericho." *Ironwood:* "The Ravine," "She Didn't Even Wave," "The Expectant Father," "The German Army, Russia, 1943." *Michigan Quarterly Review:* "Talking to His Reflection in a Shallow Pond." *Ms.:* "29 (A Dream in Two Parts)," "The Ravine." *Paris Review:* "Nothing but Color," "Killing Floor." *Virginia Quarterly Review:* "Guadalajara Hospital."

FOR THE GHOSTS

ACKNOWLEDGMENTS

I wish to thank the John Simon Guggenheim Memorial Foundation, The Radcliffe Institute, and the Massachusetts Arts and Humanities Foundation, without whose help this book might never have been finished.

CONTENTS

KILLING FLOOR

KILLING FLOOR

1. Russia, 1927

On the day the sienna-skinned man
held my shoulders between his spade-shaped hands,
easing me down into the azure water of Jordan,
I woke ninety-three million miles from myself,
Lev Davidovich Bronstein,
shoulder-deep in the Volga,
while the cheap dye of my black silk shirt darkened the water.

My head wet, water caught in my lashes.
Am I blind?
I rub my eyes, then wade back to shore,
undress and lie down,
until Stalin comes from his place beneath the birch tree.
He folds my clothes
and I button myself in my marmot coat,
and together we start the long walk back to Moscow.
He doesn't ask, *what did you see in the river?*,
but I hear the hosts of a man drowning in water and holiness,
the castrati voices I can't recognize,
skating on knives, from trees, from air
on the thin ice of my last night in Russia.
Leon Trotsky. Bread.
I want to scream, but silence holds my tongue
with small spade-shaped hands
and only this comes, so quietly

Stalin has to press his ear to my mouth:
I have only myself. Put me on the train.
I won't look back.

2. Mexico, 1940

At noon today, I woke from a nightmare:
my friend Jacques ran toward me with an ax,
as I stepped from the train in Alma-Ata.
He was dressed in yellow satin pants and shirt.
A marigold in winter.
When I held out my arms to embrace him,
he raised the ax and struck me at the neck,
my head fell to one side, hanging only by skin.
A river of sighs poured from the cut.

3. Mexico, August 20, 1940

The machine-gun bullets
hit my wife in the legs,
then zigzagged up her body.
I took the shears, cut open her gown
and lay on top of her for hours.
Blood soaked through my clothes
and when I tried to rise, I couldn't.

I wake then. Another nightmare.
I rise from my desk, walk to the bedroom

and sit down at my wife's mirrored vanity.
I rouge my cheeks and lips,
stare at my bone-white, speckled egg of a face:
lined and empty.
I lean forward and see Jacques's reflection.
I half-turn, smile, then turn back to the mirror.
He moves from the doorway,
lifts the pickax
and strikes the top of my head.
My brain splits.
The pickax keeps going
and when it hits the tile floor,
it flies from his hands,
a black dove on whose back I ride,
two men, one cursing,
the other blessing all things:
Lev Davidovich Bronstein,
I step from Jordan without you.

NOTHING BUT COLOR

For Yukio Mishima

I didn't write Etsuko,
I sliced her open.
She was carmine inside
like a sea bass
and empty.
No viscera, nothing but color.
I love you like that, boy.
I pull the kimono down around your shoulders
and kiss you.
Then you let it fall open.
Each time, I cut you a little
and when you leave, I take the piece,
broil it, dip it in ginger sauce
and eat it. It burns my mouth so.
You laugh, holding me belly-down
with your body.
So much hurting to get to this moment,
when I'm beneath you,
wanting it to go on and to end.

At midnight, you say *see you tonight*
and I answer *there won't be any tonight*,
but you just smile, swing your sweater
over your head and tie the sleeves around your neck.
I hear you whistling long after you disappear
down the subway steps,

as I walk back home, my whole body tingling.
I undress
and put the bronze sword on my desk
beside the crumpled sheet of rice paper.
I smooth it open
and read its single sentence:
I meant to do it.
No. It should be common and feminine
like *I can't go on sharing him,*
or something to imply that.
Or the truth:
that I saw in myself
the five signs of the decay of the angel
and you were holding on, watching and free,
that I decided to go out
with the pungent odor
of this cold and consuming passion in my nose: death.
Now, I've said it. That vulgar word
that drags us down to the worms, sightless, predestined.
Goddamn you, boy.
Nothing I said mattered to you;
that bullshit about Etsuko or about killing myself.
I tear the note, then burn it.
The alarm clock goes off. 5:45 A.M.
I take the sword and walk into the garden.
I look up. The sun, the moon,
two round teeth rock together

and the light of one chews up the other.
I stab myself in the belly,
wait, then stab myself again. Again.
It's snowing. I'll turn to ice,
but I'll burn anyone who touches me.
I start pulling my guts out,
those red silk cords,
spiraling skyward,
and I'm climbing them
past the moon and the sun,
past darkness
into white.
I mean to live.

LESSON, LESSON

I draw a circle on a paper bag
with the only crayon you've ever had
and hold it above the cot.
You laugh. So the sun ain't green.
You not supposed to know yet.
Just pretend maybe won't be
another little gimme-fill-my-belly
next year while you out in the fields.
Hear me. You imagine real good
because your daddy a hammer.
Hard-time nail in his pants.
He feel wood beneath him,
he got to drive it home.

JERICHO

The question mark in my belly kicks me
as I push back the sheet, watching you undress.
You put on the black mask and lie on your side.
I open the small sack of peppermint sticks
you always bring and take one out.
I suck it as you rub my shoulders, breasts,
then with one hand, round the hollow beneath,
carved by seven months of pregnancy,
stopping when your palm covers my navel.
You groan as I slide the peppermint across my lips.

So I'm just fifteen, but I've seen others like you:
afraid, apologizing because they need something
maybe nobody else does.
You candy man, handing out the money, the sweets,
ashamed to climb your ladder of trouble.
Don't be. Make it to the top.
You'll find a ram's horn there.
Blow it seven times, yell goddamn
and watch the miniature hells below you
all fall down.

THE MORTICIAN'S TWELVE-YEAR-OLD SON

Lady, when you were alive
I'd see you on the streets,
the long green dress with the velvet flower
sewn dead center between your breasts
so tightly I could never get a look inside.

Now the gas lamps half-light the table,
washing the sheet that covers you with shadows.
A few strands of your dyed red hair
hang nearly to the floor,
as if all your blood had run there to hide.

I lift the sheet, rub the mole on your cheek
and it comes off black and oily on my hand.
I bend over your breasts and sing,
love, sister, is just a kiss away.
I cover each nipple with my mouth.
Tonight, just a kiss away.

THE GERMAN ARMY, RUSSIA, 1943

For twelve days,
I drilled through Moscow ice
to reach paradise,
that white tablecloth, set with a plate
that's cracking bit by bit
like the glassy air, like me.
I know I'll fly apart soon,
the pieces of me so light they float.
The Russians burned their crops,
rather than feed our army.
Now they strike us against each other like dry rocks
and set us on fire with a hunger
nothing can feed.
Someone calls me and I look up.
It's Hitler.
I imagine eating his terrible, luminous eyes.
Brother, he says.
I stand up, tie the rags tighter around my feet.
I hear my footsteps running after me,
but I am already gone.

TALKING TO HIS REFLECTION IN A SHALLOW POND

For Yasunari Kawabata

Chrysanthemum and nightshade:
I live on them,
though air is what I need.
I wish I could breath like you,
asleep, or even awake,
just resting your head
on the pillow wrapped in black crepe
that I brought you from Sweden.
I hoped you'd die,
your mouth open, lips dry and split,
and red like pomegranate seeds.
But now, I only want you to suffer.
I drop a stone in the pond
and it sinks through you.
Japan isn't sliding into the Pacific
this cool April morning, you are.
Yasunari Kawabata, I'm talking to you;
just drop like that stone
through your own reflection.
You stretch your lean hands toward me
and I take them.
Water covers my face, my whole head,
as I inhale myself:
cold, very cold.

11

Suddenly, I pull back.
For a while, I watch you struggle,
then I start walking back to my studio.
But something is wrong.
There's water everywhere
and you're standing above me.
I stare up at you from the still, clear water.
You open your mouth and I open mine.
We both speak slowly.
Brother, you deserve to suffer,
You deserve the best:
this moment, death without end.

29 (A DREAM IN TWO PARTS)

1.

Night, that old woman, jabs the sun
with a pitchfork,
and dyes the cheesecloth sky blue–violet,
as I sit at the kitchen table,
bending small pieces of wire in hoops.
You come in naked.
No. Do it yourself.

2.

I'm a nine-year-old girl,
skipping beside a single hoop of daylight.
I hear your voice.
I start running. You lift me in your arms.
I holler. The little girl turns.
Her hoop rolls out of sight.
Something warm seeps through my gown onto my belly.
She never looks back.

SHE DIDN'T EVEN WAVE

For Marilyn Monroe

I buried Mama in her wedding dress
and put gloves on her hands,
but I couldn't do much about her face,
blue-black and swollen,
so I covered it with a silk scarf.
I hike my dress up to my thighs
and rub them,
watching you tip the mortuary fan back and forth.
Hey. Come on over. Cover me all up
like I was never here. Just never.
Come on. I don't know why I talk like that.
It was a real nice funeral. Mama's.
I touch the rhinestone heart pinned to my blouse.
Honey, let's look at it again.
See. It's bright like the lightning that struck her.

I walk outside
and face the empty house.
You put your arms around me. Don't.
Let me wave goodbye.
Mama never got a chance to do it.
She was walking toward the barn
when it struck her. I didn't move;
I just stood at the screen door.
Her whole body was light.
I'd never seen anything so beautiful.

I remember how she cried in the kitchen
a few minutes before.
She said, *God. Married.*
I don't believe it, Jean, I won't.
He takes and takes and you just give.
At the door, she held out her arms
and I ran to her.
She squeezed me so tight:
I was all short of breath.
And she said, *don't do it.*
In ten years, your heart will be eaten out
and you'll forgive him, or some other man, even that
and it will kill you.
Then she walked outside.
And I kept saying, I've got to, Mama,
hug me again. Please don't go.

ICE

breaks up in obelisks on the river,
as I stand beside your grave.
I tip my head back.
Above me, the same sky you loved,
that shawl of cotton wool,
frozen around the shoulders of Minnesota.
I'm cold and so far from Texas
and my father, who gave me to you.
I was twelve, a Choctaw, a burden.
A woman, my father said, raising my skirt.
Then he showed you the roll of green gingham,
stained red, that I'd tried to crush to powder
with my small hands. I close my eyes,

and it is March 1866 again.
I'm fourteen, wearing a white smock.
I straddle the rocking horse you made for me
and stroke the black mane cut from my own hair.
Sunrise hugs you from behind,
as you walk through the open door
and lay the velvet beside me.
I give you the ebony box
with the baby's skull inside
and you set it on your work table,
comb your pale blond hair with one hand,
then nail it shut.
When the new baby starts crying, I cover my ears,

watching as you lift him from the cradle
and lay him on the pony-skin rug.
I untie the red scarf, knotted at my throat,
climb off the horse and bend over you.
I slip the scarf around your neck,
and pull it tight, remembering:
I strangled the other baby,
laid her on your stomach while you were asleep.
You break my hold and pull me to the floor.
I scratch you, bite your lips, your face,
then you cry out,
and I open and close my hands
around a row of bear teeth.

I open my eyes.
I wanted you then and now,
and I never let you know.
I kiss the headstone.
Tonight, wake me like always.
Talk and I'll listen,
while you lie on the pallet
resting your arms behind your head,
telling me about the wild rice in the marshes
and the empty .45 you call *Grace of God* that keeps you alive,
as we slide forward, without bitterness, decade by decade,
becoming transparent. Everlasting.

THE RAVINE

I wake, sweating, reach for your rosary and drop it.
I roll over on the straw and sit up. It's light out.
I pull on my pants, slip into my rope sandals
and go outside, where you sit
against a sack of beans.
I touch the chicken feathers
stuck to the purple splotches of salve on your stomach.
Your eyes, two tiny bowls of tar
set deep in your skull, stare straight ahead
and your skin is almost the color of your eyes,
because Death pressed his black face against yours.
I put our daughter in your lap,
lift you both and walk to the ravine's edge.
I step over —

— the years fly up in my face like a fine gray dust.
I'm twenty. I buy you with matches, a mirror and a rifle.
You don't talk. While I ride the mule downhill,
you walk beside me in a blue cotton dress.
Your flat Indian face shines with boar grease.
Your wide feet sink deep in the spring mud.
You raise your hands to shade your eyes
from the sudden explosion of sunlight
through the umber clouds.
In that brightness, you separate into five stained-glass women.
Four of you are floating north, south, east and west.
I reach out, shatter you in each direction.

I start to fall, catch myself,
get off the mule and make you ride.
You cry silently, ashamed to let me walk.
At bottom, you look back.
I keep going. Up a few yards,
I strip two thin pieces of bark off a tamarisk tree,
and we chew on them, sweetening the only way home.

GUADALAJARA CEMETERY

You sort the tin paintings
and lay your favorite in my lap.
Then you stroke my bare feet
as I lean against a tombstone.
It's time to cross the border
and cut your throat with two knives:
your wife, your son.
I won't try to stop you.
A cow with a mouth at both ends
chews hell going and coming.
I never asked less.
You, me, these withered flowers,
so many hearts tied in a knot,
given and taken away.

GUADALAJARA HOSPITAL

I watch the orderly stack the day's dead:
men on one cart, women on the other.
You sit two feet away, sketching
and drinking tequila.
I raise my taffeta skirt above the red garter,
take out the pesos
and lay them beside you.
I don't hold out on you.
I shove my hand under my skirt,
find the damp ten-dollar bill.
You're on top. You call the shots.
You said we'd make it here and we have.
I make them pay for it.

Later, we walk close,
smoking from one cigarette
until it's gone. I take your arm.
Next stop *end of the line.* You pull me to you
and push your tongue deep in my mouth.
I bite it. We struggle. You slap me.
I lean over the hood of the car.
You clamp a handkerchief between your teeth,
take the pesos and ten-dollar bill from your pocket
and tear them up.
Then you get in the car
and I slide in beside you.

When we finally cross the border,
I stare out the back window.
The Virgin Mary's back there
in her husband Mendoza's workroom.
She's sitting on a tall stool,
her black lace dress rolled up above her knees,
the red pumps dangling from her feet,
while he puts the adz to a small coffin;
a psalm of hammer and emptiness
only the two of them understand.
You say, *sister, breathe with me.*
We're home, now, home.
But I reach back, back through the window.
Virgin Mary, help me. Save me.
Tear me apart with your holy, invisible hands.

THE KID

My sister rubs the doll's face in mud,
then climbs through the truck window.
She ignores me as I walk around it,
hitting the flat tires with an iron rod.
The old man yells for me to help hitch the team,
but I keep walking around the truck, hitting harder,
until my mother calls.
I pick up a rock and throw it at the kitchen window,
but it falls short.
The old man's voice bounces off the air like a ball
I can't lift my leg over.

I stand beside him, waiting, but he doesn't look up
and I squeeze the rod, raise it, his skull splits open.
Mother runs toward us. I stand still,
get her across the spine as she bends over him.
I drop the rod and take the rifle from the house.
Roses are red, violets are blue,
one bullet for the black horse, two for the brown.
They're down quick. I spit, my tongue's bloody;
I've bitten it. I laugh, remember the one out back.
I catch her climbing from the truck, shoot.
The doll lands on the ground with her.
I pick it up, rock it in my arms.
Yeah. I'm Jack, Hogarth's son.
I'm nimble, I'm quick.

In the house, I put on the old man's best suit
and his patent leather shoes.
I pack my mother's satin nightgown
and my sister's doll in the suitcase.
Then I go outside and cross the fields to the highway.
I'm fourteen. I'm a wind from nowhere.
I can break your heart.

ALMOST GROWN

I swing up on the sideboard of the old car. I'm wearing
the smell of hay better than I do these starched coveralls,
my dead father's shirt, patched under each arm, and the
underwear I bought especially for today. Mother says nothing,
just watches me and sucks on her unlit pipe. My sister,
still too young to get away, wipes away a few tears with the end
of her blue apron. The red bitch runs behind yapping, then
veers into the charred field, where she chases her tail
and, building speed, makes wider and wider circles, until
she is just a streak of fire, finally burning herself to a quick stop.

I get off at the feed store. The old men playing cards ignore me.
It's Saturday afternoon. I carry the cardboard box that holds my
things under one arm, swinging the other. I see Jake the Bootlegger's
car, parked in front of the café. When I'm close, the sun
strikes its gray steel with a hammer and I have to shade my eyes
from the glare. I grope for the door, then stagger inside. The
cooler rattles a welcome. Mae, the waitress, hollers from the
kitchen, but I can't make out what she says. I sit on a stool with
the box propped up beside me.

Suddenly, Jake comes out and Mae follows him. He winks at me.
I stare through Mae's sheer nylon blouse at her lace bra. She
takes my order and I watch her as she walks to the far end of the
counter, where Jake sits, waiting, twisting the long gold chain
of his watch. I grunt with satisfaction. Good I moved, left the
farm to finish dying without me. I take out my ten-dollar bill,

rub it, feeling all the things I can buy with it: a striped tie,
one more box of cigars, a room for a week at the hotel. Hell!
It's great. Two more days and I start work at the gas station.
I take a big bite out of the hamburger Mae has set on the counter.

Jake gets up, Mae reaches for him. He shakes his head and
walks outside. She goes into the kitchen, and soon I hear her crying.
I hesitate, then follow her. She's lying on a cot, jammed against
the wall. I bend over her and she lifts her hand and touches me
the way no one ever has. I'm clumsy, but it gets done, same as
anything, I guess. She shoves me, cursing. Money, she wants
money. I'm nervous, I clutch the ten, then throw it at her. I run,
grabbing my box. In the street again, the heat, my empty pockets
heavy, as if filled with coins. At the gas station, I slip into the
Men's room and bolt the door. I sit on the dusty toilet and lean
back against the tank. Shit! I'm not through yet. I heard this
somewhere and it's true, it's got to be: you can't tell a shotgun
or a man what to do.

THE EXPECTANT FATHER

The skin of my mouth, chewed raw, tastes good.
I get up, cursing, and find the bottle of Scotch.
My mouth burns as darkess, lifting her skirt,
reveals daylight, a sleek left ankle.
The woman calls. I don't answer.
I imagine myself coming up to my own door,
holding a small reed basket in my arms.
Inside it, there is a child,
with clay tablets instead of hands,
and my name is written on each one.
The woman calls me again and I go to her.
She reaches for me, but I move away.
I frown, pulling back the covers to look at her.
So much going on outside;
the walls could cave in on us any time, any time.
I bring my face down
where the child's head should be and press hard.
I feel pain, she's pulling my hair.
I rise up, finally, and back away from the bed,
while she turns on her side
and drags her legs up to her chest.
I wait for her to cry,
then go into the kitchen.
I fix a Scotch and sit down at the table.
In six months, it is coming, in six months,
and I have no weapon against it.

SLEEP LIKE A HAMMER

I rub the hammer I use to slaughter stock
with coconut oil,
while you sit, staring at your feet, clucking,
though you've bent your head
so I can't see your lips.
The night the barn burned down,
I was crazy for help,
but you just sat on the porch
with your shoes in your lap.
I grabbed them and ran
and when I threw them into the fire,
you went in after them.
I had to drag you out
and beat out the flames.
Now you just sit,
every so often lifting your hands
as if they were holding broken glass,
and I don't know what to do, father,
I know you're thinking about your shoes
and I go on oiling, oiling,
because it's not good to let blood
harden in the cracks,
though the cows, the hogs don't care,
even I don't. I just worry like a woman.
I need something to do.
When I was fifteen, you took the pregnant hound
hunting at flood time and she didn't come back.

You said she was no good anyway
and I kicked you hard.
You took the shovel from the barn
and smashed my leg. I still limp.
I raise the hammer.
I hear my wife yelling.
She's running toward me,
bucket in one hand, the eggs in it
sloshing over the top;
huge white drops of water.
But she's in another country.
There's only you. Me.
When I bring the hammer down,
your toes splay out, snap off like burned bacon.
Your lips pull back
and your tongue drifts over your teeth
and I'm moving up to your hands, shoulders, neck, face.
Lord, moving up.

FATHER AND SON

THE MAN:
The priest and the old women
drag themselves over the hill,
as if bearing up a tiny coffin.
I look at you and the boy,
stretched out on the ground,
then back at them.
Their feet catch fire in the sunset.
Night is coming, shouldering a sack of misdeeds
that glow in the dark. Night and the carnival.
Night and the Devil.
I wipe the sweat from my face
and put on my Devil costume:
red shirt, red pants and the cotton mask.
I get the whip I keep under the pile of rocks
and strike the air with it.
When you wake, turning over on your back,
you hiss and hit your chest three times.
Keep quiet, woman. I strike the air again;
its ten-year-old hands, genitals, feet.

THE WOMAN:
I get up, pull on my burlap dress
and lift the lid off the papier-mâché coffin
you've laid across two sawhorses.
In it lies a porcelain doll,

wearing a baptismal dress.
I was pregnant when I told you
burn a doll each year
and the tenth year the boy will catch fire,
will burn away, not even leaving smoke behind.
You believed it, the way you believe
misery's a clock nobody can't walk,
that it's half past I've got,
or a quarter to got to get a shoe, get a shoe,
before the price of leather goes up.
But I say misery's another man's child.
Like this one. Francisco's son, not yours.
Francisco I took to bed,
Francisco who left Villa in 1917
and left me, too, there in the camp
and who, when you finally caught him,
heard my name and turned his pockets inside out.
He's coming tonight, after confession,
one ride on the ferris wheel
and a few drinks. He'll come.

THE MAN:
I never believed anything you said.
You had two men who now are nothing but shadows,
and soon only black like this doll's sockets.
That's what I believe in, the black.

Only the black forgets, so I wait.
I tend your garden of evil and watch it ripen.
Wake the boy. Go on, call him: Baby Bones, Baby Bones.
When you shake him, his head twists,
fear's wood slides under his fingernails,
he turns his round face to me and I almost reach for him.
When he gets up, I give him his costume: red shirt,
red pants, a mask.
He puts them on and I start the fire.
I never believed anything you said.

THE WOMAN:

The boy's an ape. If you look at him all the time
like I do, you see there's nothing human about him.
Francisco knows: that's why he comes,
to see for himself how his little ape grows and grows
like an ear of rainbow-colored corn,
after twelve long months of invisible rain,
rain that burns.
Sin: eat with it, sleep with it,
dress it up like the Devil.
He's still an ape.

THE MAN:

You don't know, woman. You don't know.
Everyday he's here, another man's son,

calling me father, making mud bricks with me.
Honor thy father, they say, but I say curse him.
Son of a bitch and son of a bastard,
that's what a father is. I tell him that.
Don't call me father, I say. I'm not,
you know who is.
I used to have you beat him for it
Father, he'd cry, *help me.*
Always the same.
Francisco won't come.
I saw him yesterday, in the village,
spitting blood again. And there, at his throat
the eruption of hair you find so beautiful.
I wanted to press my face in it, to bite deep,
but I held back.
He spat one last time, right at my feet,
and he walked away with his donkey
and one chicken in a cage.
I could have killed him.
Instead, my rage stabs at his back
again and again, and misses,
because it is going into the black,
where nothing touches nothing.
It starts with a toe and crawls up,
eating the shadow,
its fragments of sentences, match-heads, hope.
Here's the coffin. Go ahead, burn it.

You throw it into the fire.
I laugh. The boy dances and I follow him,
'round and 'round, two black tops on fire,
spinning under a sky full of firecrackers and stars,
letting fall a few handkerchiefs of light.

I CAN'T GET STARTED

For Ira Hayes

1. Saturday Night

A coyote eats chunks of the moon,
the night hen's yellow egg,
while I lie drunk, in a ditch.
Suddenly, a huge combat boot
punches a hole through the sky
and falls toward me.
I wave my arms. Get back.
It keeps coming.

2. Sunday Morning

I stumble out of the ditch
and make it to the shack.
I shoot a few holes in the roof,
then stare at the paper clippings of Iwo Jima.
I remember raising that rag
of red, white and blue,
afraid that if I let go, I'd live.
The bullets never touched me.
Nothing touches me.

Around noon, I make a cup of coffee
and pour a teaspoon of pepper in it
to put the fire out.
I hum between sips

and when I finish, I hug myself.
I'm burning from the bottom up,
a bottle of flesh,
kicked across the hardwood years.
I pass gin and excuses from hand to mouth,
but it's me. It's me.
I'm the one dirty habit
I just can't break.

HE KEPT ON BURNING

1. Spain, 1929

In the café, the chandelier hangs from the ceiling
by a thick rope. I'm seventeen, still a boy.
I put my hand in my lap and twist my class
ring 'round and 'round the little finger. The Basque,
toad in torn breeches and burlap vest, plays the guitar.
I look toward the stairs. The man is there, his hand
on the wooden railing. He's naked, except for the white
kimono with black cranes painted on it, and the brown pumps
with taps on each heel. I take a slice of salami, swallow
without chewing much. He comes to me, shaking his hips
as the guitar grows louder, leans down and lets me rub
a glassful of wine across his hard, rose-colored nipples.
Then he turns, taps his feet and the others clap their hands.
I take the cheese knife, slap it down on the table. He stomps,
right foot, left, one-two, one-two-three, back toward me on the
third step. He laughs, touches my lips and I sing,
Und der haifisch der hat zahne. The others watch me.
Trembling, I move to the door. I'm not one of you.
I back into the street, cursing. I slam my fist against the wall.
It doesn't bleed. The door opens, the kimono is thrown outside.
I pick it up, smell it. On the train back to Germany, that smell
and a voice whispering, dance with me baby,
all night long.

2. Buchenwald, 1945

Joseph, you move beneath the blankets. I uncover you
and hold the glass of brandy to your mouth. Your eyes open.
Wake up, Jew, drink with me, eat some of the fine German
cake my mother sent. You take the glass and drink.
I put a small piece of cake in my mouth. I taste something:
a man, a country, Schmuel Meyer, Jenny Towler, Alphonse
Glite, seven children, metal. I squeeze my eyes shut. We
leave today. Am I shaking? I do shake, don't I. I stare
through the window at the last group of prisoners,
patchwork quilt, embroidered with the letters SS.
It is drizzling now four days and each man, cloth dipped
in useless dye, is running into the mud at his feet.
I turn my hands up; the palms are almost smooth.
I hear the shots. I keep looking at my hands.
When I was seventeen, Joseph, when I was seventeen,
I put out a fire, but it kept on burning.

3. Peru, 1955

Midnight bleeds through the window
as you walk to the table
and drink warm beer from a tin mug.
I sniff the sausages you've laid beside the boiled eggs
and hard bread. Are they as old as that time
I told you *come with me*? You'd love me, you said.

Yes, you and guilt, tabernacle of gold teeth
and the cantor inside singing over and over, *thou shalt not.*
I take your wrist; so thin, Joseph. Suicide? — no.
There's always the boy, always,
and a kimono that smells like orange blossoms.
And hurting; twenty-six years on a razor's edge.
And I want more. More.

THE WOMAN WHO KNEW TOO MUCH

I plait Carmen's hair tightly,
smelling the odor of straw
she takes with her everywhere.
Then I fasten the earrings in her ears,
the ones I made
that are orange,
like the inside of her mouth
when she's been drinking rum.

When the killer comes for her,
because she won't fight,
because she knows too much —
our guns, our weakness —
she offers him rum.
His mustache of two cigars gleams.

Later, I bury her,
then slip down into the valley
to wait for reinforcements.
I eat the yams she fried for me
and when I'm done,
I feel as if I've been sleeping.

Near sunrise, I see them:
five men and two women.
They want freedom on their own terms.
But it isn't like that.

They'll find out as Carmen did.
I go to meet them.
They think they've brought me everything I need
and now I'll tell them like all the others
that they are right.
Line up, you bastards,
so I can take a closer look.
Tonight I let my woman die.
She also had arms, legs, fingers,
all the unimportant things.
I don't want to forget. I won't let you.
Go ahead, strut around,
talk, fire your guns.
But don't tell me about freedom.
Just let me see his face.

THE SINGERS

1.

You lift a piece of meat to your mouth
with the silver fork
you took from the burning house.
It glitters in your hand,
a sliver of light on mud.
Don't leave me, woman, not now.
I smell the shit odor of fear again
like the night five years ago
when I crossed the Rio Grande into Texas.
The Carranzistas had killed Zapata
and they'd kill me too, if I stayed in Chihuahua.
But half a mile in, I saw him:
Zapata on the ground in front of me.
He bowed and danced slowly around his sombrero,
and the bullet holes in his body,
black, eight-pointed stars,
gave off a luminous darkness.

Back in Mexico, I don't remember riding,
only standing beside my horse
outside a whitewashed house.
When I looked through the window,
I saw you and your father, Indian, like me,
sitting at a table, bare, except for a silver fork.
Help me, I said. *I rode with Zapata.*

But neither of you moved.
You started singing: *Zapata, Zapata, your blood is so red.*
Zapata, Zapata, you're dead.
Who's at the window, a ghost, a ghost, only a ghost.
And when I lifted my hands,
they were transparent,
my bones, colorless light.
I struck the window,
they shattered
and I smelled fear again. I could see it:
the black outline of a horse on its hind legs,
a zero burning on its belly,
burning for me, Rosebud Morales.
I screamed, screamed my name
until I came back to myself
and could see my hands, their russet skin,
wrapping some straw in a ball.
I set it afire and threw it into the house.
When you ran out, I grabbed you.
You stabbed me with the fork, but I held on.
You kept singing while your father burned.

2.

You wrap the Spanish Bible you can't read
in your shawl,
then you start running.

But I catch you by your braids,
drag you to the cooking fire and push your head in it.
When I let go, you stagger up
wearing a halo of flames.
Come on, sing with me: *Zapata, Zapata, your blood is so red.*
Sing, goddamnit. You fall.
The shadow of a train rises from your body
and lightning zigzags from the smokestack.
The smokestack is a man. Zapata. I raise my pistol.
I'm not afraid of any sonofabitch on two feet.
I fire, then jam the barrel in my mouth.
Not even you, motherfucker, not even you.

PENTECOST

For Myself

Rosebud Morales, my friend,
before you deserted,
you'd say anyone can kill an Indian
and forget it the same instant,
that it will happen to me, Emiliano Zapata.
But my men want more corn for tortillas,
more pigs, more chickens, more chilis
and land.
If I haven't got a gun or a knife,
I'll fight with a pitchfork or a hoe,
to take them from the bosses,
those high-flying birds,
with the pomade glistening on their hair,
as they promenade into their coffins.
And if I'm killed, if we're all killed right now,
we'll go on, the true Annunciation.

Rosebud, how beautiful this day is.
I'm riding to meet Guajardo.
He'll fight with me now,
against Carranza.
When I get to the hacienda, it's quiet.
Not many soldiers,
a sorrel horse, its reins held
by a woman in a thin, white American dress
and Guajardo standing on a balcony.

I get off my horse and start up the steps.
My legs burn, my chest,
my jaw, my head.
There's a hill in front of me;
it's slippery, I have to use my hands to climb it.
At the top, it's raining fire and blood
on rows and rows of black corn.
Machetes are scattered everywhere.
I grab one and start cutting the stalks.
When they hit the ground,
they turn into men.
I yell at them.
You're damned in the cradle,
in the grave, even in Heaven.
Dying doesn't end anything.
Get up. Swing those machetes.
You can't steal a man's glory
without a goddamned fight.
Boys, take the land, take it; it's yours.
If you suffer in the grave,
you can kill from it.

THE GILDED MAN

In 1561, on an expedition down the Marañon and
Amazon to find El Dorado, Lope de Aguirre killed
Urzúa, the leader of the expedition, then scores of
others. He declared rebellion against Spain and set
out to conquer Peru, *con el alma en los dientes*, with
his soul between his teeth.

1. The Orinoco, 1561

For a while today, the rafts almost float side by side.
The river is as smooth and soft
as the strip of emerald velvet
sewn around the hem of your dress, my daughter.
I call you Vera Cruz,
because you are the true cross
from which I hang by ropes of gold.
The word *father*, a spear of dark brown hair,
enters my side and disintegrates,
leaving me whole again,
smelling of quinces and gunpowder
and your stale, innocent breath.
What is it?
you whisper. I take your hand
and we walk into the jungle.
I watch you raise your dress, bend,
then tear your petticoat with your teeth.
You fold the torn cloth
and slide it between your legs.
Then you hold out your bloody hands

and I wipe them on my shirt,
already red from fighting.
Urzúa is dead. Guzmán is dead. There is no Spain.
I'm hunting El Dorado, the Gilded Man.
When I catch him. I'll cut him up.
I'll start with his feet
and give them to you to wear as earrings.
Talk to me.
I hear nothing but the monkeys squealing above me.
I point my arquebus at a silhouette in the trees, and fire.
For a moment, I think it's you falling toward me,
your dress shredding to sepia light.
I drop the arquebus and stretch out my hands.
Fall, darling, fall into me.
Lope de Aguirre. I hear my name
as I lift you in my arms.
Daughter. Beautiful.
You weigh no more than ashes.

2. Barquisimeto, Venezuela, October 27, 1561

Today it rained vengefully and hard
and my men deserted me.
My kingdom was as close
as calling it by name. Peru.
I braid your hair, daughter,
as you kneel with your head in my lap.

I talk softly, stopping to press your face to my chest.
Vera Cruz. Listen. My heart is speaking.
I am the fishes, the five loaves.
The women, the men I killed simply ate me.
There is no dying, only living in death.
I was their salvation.
I am absolved by their hunger.
El Dorado, the kingdom of gold,
is only a tapestry I wove from their blood.
Stand up. My enemies will kill me
and they won't be merciful with you.
I unsheathe my dagger. Your mouth opens.
I can't hear you. I want to. Tell me you love me.
You cover your mouth with your hands.
I stab you, then fall beside your body.
Vera Cruz. See my skin covered with gold dust
and tongues of flame,
transfigured by the pentecost of my own despair.
I, Aguirre the wanderer, Aguirre the traitor,
the Gilded Man.
Does God think that because it rains in torrents
I am not to go to Peru and destroy the world?
God. The boot heel an inch above your head is mine.
God, say your prayers.